"We went into this together, and we're coming out at the end together."

- Barbara Stanwyck as Phyllis Dietrichson in
DOUBLE INDEMNITY (1944)

NEITHER HERE NOIR THERE

Neither Here Noir There

A play by Bambi Everson

EVERSON COLEMAN

NEW YORK

CAUTION: Professionals and amateurs are hereby warned that the play represented in this book is subject to a royalty. It is fully protected under the copyright laws of the United States of America, and of all countries covered by the International Copyright Union (including the Dominion of Canada and the rest of the British Commonwealth), and of all countries covered by the Pan-American Copyright Convention and the Universal Copyright Convention, and of all countries with which the United States has reciprocal copyright relations. All rights, including professional, amateur, motion picture, recitation, lecturing, public reading, radio broadcasting, television, video or sound taping, all other forms of mechanical or electronic reproductions, information storage and retrieval systems and photocopying, and the rights of translation into foreign languages, are strictly reserved. Particular emphasis is laid upon the question of public readings, permission for which must be secured from the Author or their authorized representative. We'll probably say yes, but please ask.

Exceptions are made in the case of brief quotations embodied in critical reviews, educational or scholarly purposes and certain artistic and other noncommercial uses permitted by copyright law. This is a work of fiction. Any resemblance to actual events or persons, living or dead, is entirely coincidental.

All inquiries concerning rights should be sent via email to bambieverson@gmail.com.

For performance of any music, songs, arrangements, and recordings mentioned in this volume, which are protected by copyright, the permission of the copyright owners must be obtained; or other songs and recordings in the public domain substituted.

NEITHER HERE NOIR THERE Copyright © 2016 Bambi Everson

UNPLUGGED Copyright © 2020 Bambi Everson

Editing, cover art and layout by Frank Coleman
Published by Everson/Coleman

First Edition: September 2022

All rights reserved.

ISBN: 978-1-7375411-3-4

AUTHOR'S NOTE

Writers gather their ideas from a myriad of influences. This play was an homage to my dad, William K. Everson, who exposed me to film noir at a very young age. By the time I was eight, I knew that bad girls never win, and lived my life accordingly. I also wrote this play to honor a longstanding friendship, which has encompassed years of trading "bad relationship stories."

I went back to school, Empire State College, 37 years after completing high school. In my second year there, my advisor thought I might enjoy a playwriting class. I thought she was overestimating my abilities, but acquiesced. It turned out to be a major turning point in my life. Thank you, Lucy Winner, for having more faith in me than I had in myself.

Lynda Crawford's playwriting lab was the most fun I ever had in or out of school. NOIR was my first attempt at writing a full-length piece. I wrote a 10-minute play, HOLDOUT, the semester before.

For the first public reading at Empire State, I was so fortunate to have Nick Lawson, Tammy Caddell, and Aimee Howard, as Michael, Alice, and Maxie, respectively. Tammy is British, and I saw the character and the relationship in a new light.

When you write a character that is loosely based on yourself, it is a sheer delight to find an actor who finds a different and unexpected road that results in the same destination. All three actors exceeded my expectations.

When the opportunity arose to have a full production, I had a minor dilemma. Manhattan Rep was a non-Equity theater, and all my actors were Equity members. I had to switch gears.

I was fortunate to meet Annie Gaarder while at school. I saw Annie as a better version of myself, and did some rewrites to accommodate her talents.

Elanna White is an actor I have known since she was 8 years old. She is one of the most dependable and versatile actors I know. I have always followed her work with a bit of vicarious parental pride.

It was actually my BFF, Michael, who suggested former sit-com actor John Femia after seeing him in another of my readings. We both felt he had the same self-deprecating humor and odd ball charm needed for the character.

Finding a director was a new challenge for me as I was just starting out as a producer/playwright. I brought my friend, Elissa Middleton, aboard. She was already an accomplished actor, I knew she understood the genre, and was sticking her toe in the water as a director.

I am so grateful to all of them for bringing NOIR to the stage, and for the dozens of life lessons I learned about self-producing that I took to heart. Having written over 20 plays since, it is nice to look back on this one, and think, "Maybe this playwriting thing wasn't such an ill-advised idea after all."

This play is dedicated to the Michaels in my life. Michael Aschner, for 35+ years of inspiration and friendship, and the late Michael Schulman, my teacher and friend who never stopped telling me I could, so I finally did.

Bambi Everson
New York City, September 2022

PRODUCTION HISTORY

Reading – Empire State College, NYC, 2015
With Tammy Caddell*, Aimee Howard* and Nick Lawson*
* appearing with permission of Actors' Equity Association.

Student Production – Winthrop University, Rock Hill, SC, 2016

Full production – Manhattan Repertory Theatre, NYC, 2017
With Annie Gaarder, John Femia, and Elanna White. Directed by Elissa Middleton.

Annie Gaarder, Elanna White, and John Femia (l to r). Photo: Frank Coleman

NEITHER HERE NOIR THERE
By Bambi Everson
One act, approximately 60 minutes

CHARACTERS:

MICHAEL ALEXANDER, 30's or 40's, a recently divorced writer.
ALICE MARTIN, 30's or 40's, Michael's platonic best friend for over 20 years.
MAXIE MALONE, 20's, Michael's creation, a film noir movie siren.
DELIVERY GUY, Chinese, offstage voice
PUPPY, a dog, or a person with a dog puppet

PLACE: Alice's New York City apartment, a walkup in Queens.
TIME: The Present

SYNOPSIS:

Michael, newly divorced, broke and depressed, has taken up residence at the apartment of his best friend, Alice. Prompted by Alice, Michael begins to rework a discarded film noir novel. He soon runs into trouble when his femme fatale, Maxie Malone, comes to life with an agenda of her own – one that does not include Alice. *Blithe Spirit* meets *The Maltese Falcon*.

PRODUCTION NOTES: Chinese delivery person is just a voice, could be male or female. Same for the person using the dog puppet at the end. Quick costume changes are needed for Maxie at the beginning of Scene 2. A wig and layered clothing may be helpful.

It helps to have some knowledge of film noir style. The dialogue is stylized in places and should be delivered in classic "hard boiled" style.

The other important note is the relationship between Michael and Alice is clearly affectionate, yet platonic. Michael's journey is about self-acceptance without a romantic relationship to validate it.

SPECIAL THANKS

My name may be on the front, but I never would have done anything without those who had my back. Special thanks to all our friends who contributed to our first production of NEITHER HERE NOIR THERE. Truly, it could not have happened without your support!

Michael Aschner
Anne & John Attanas
Jean Austin
Sheila Bryans
Ana Cerro
Angela Cooper
Lynda Crawford
Katherine Desmond
Barbara Finnegan
Pat & Karen Finnegan
Ruth Gelfand
Deirdre Hammer
Danny Koch
Annemarie Lawson
Diana McGinniss
Elissa Middleton
Tim Molloy
Maria Narimanidze
Gabriell DeBear Paye
Denise Reiner
Lisa Ribando
Janet Rosado
Richard Scheckman
Alison Shaiman
Eddie Shellman
Jill Shely
Betty Steinman
Jan Stern
Michele Stork
Rachel Strausberg
Christine & Will Warren
Sarah White
John Wilson
Anon Ymous

SCENE 1

ALICE MARTIN'S walk-up apartment in Queens. Obviously, this is a woman who loves movies. Her shelves are stocked with books and DVDs, and movie posters are the main décor. There are many tchotchkes. It is a cluttered, but not messy apartment – or at least it was before MICHAEL came to stay. MICHAEL is unseen, wrapped up in blankets on the living room couch. There are clothes scattered on the floor, a cup of cold coffee, some wrappers from McDonald's and other debris. The late afternoon sun is streaming through the window.

Traffic sounds from outside.

Enter ALICE. She is loaded down with on oversized purse, and groceries. She puts her bags down in the kitchen area, surveys the damage, and sighs. She puts a couple things in the fridge, the rest on the counter (or a table), goes into the living area and begins to clean up the mess. She picks up the wrappers and the coffee cup, and takes them to the kitchen. Picks up his clothes and puts them on top of his suitcase at the foot of the couch. She whips off blanket to fold it. MICHAEL is revealed in his underwear. ALICE screams! MICHAEL screams!

MICHAEL
What the fuck!?
(grabs blanket back)

ALICE
I thought you were gone!

MICHAEL
Obviously not.

ALICE
It's after 4!

MICHAEL
Your point?

ALICE
It's just... Well, I thought today you might... You want some coffee?

MICHAEL
I have coffee.

He reaches down for his cup, finds it not there, glares at her.

ALICE
There's more in the kitchen.
(Michael does not move)
I'll get it.

ALICE goes back into the kitchen and takes coffee from coffee maker and sticks it in the microwave. MICHAEL slowly sits up, still wrapped in his blanket. She hands it to him.

MICHAEL
Thanks. I'm not a morning person.
(ALICE is silent)
Afternoons aren't that hot, either.

ALICE
What can I do? It's almost 6 weeks! I'm trying to help, but frankly I'm at a loss here.

MICHAEL
Nothing. There is nothing you can do. I shouldn't have come. I wouldn't inflict me on anyone.

ALICE
I promised myself I wouldn't try to impose my timetable on you. And I don't mind you staying here. I don't! But coming home to... this, every day, is hard! Really hard! I just miss the old Michael so much.

MICHAEL
I tried to warn you. This is the Michael I never wanted you to see.

MICHAEL (cont.)
Genevieve got fed up after 5 months. And I was sleeping with her!

ALICE
I owe you. You were there for me during the whole David debacle. I wouldn't have gotten through that without you! I should have more patience. This is not my first Michael meltdown rodeo!

MICHAEL
This is different. This is not me drunk off my ass, weeping on your stoop about a married chick. This is me pulling a Felix Unger.

He speaks with a "narration voice," reciting the opening from the TV show, The Odd Couple.

MICHAEL
"On November 13th, Michael Alexander was asked to leave his place of residence - that request came from his wife..."
(singing the theme song)
Dooo do do do-do-do... Except you're not Oscar Madison, you're the Flying Nun!

ALICE
I wish! Didn't she weigh like 90 pounds?

MICHAEL
I just don't want you to wind up hating me. That would be the worst thing that could possibly happen to me. I know how you put on this happy face and let things fester... If this screws up our friendship...

ALICE
It won't. Sometimes you just have to have a little faith.

MICHAEL
Yes, Sister Bertrille.

ALICE
Actually, that's Mariel Hemmingway in "Manhattan." You should know that! Why don't you put on some clothes and take a walk with me?

MICHAEL
Outside?

ALICE
Ok... A shower, then.
(throws him a towel)

MICHAEL
I don't know who I am!

ALICE
That's ok. There have been plenty of men in my shower who haven't had a clue. I'm going to make a grilled cucumber and nutella sandwich. A specialty of the house. Want one?

MICHAEL
I'm just going to finish this coffee.

ALICE starts making sandwiches in the kitchen area.

ALICE
You have to put something in your stomach.

MICHAEL
You mean other than my heart?

ALICE
Always the poet. So, while I am here slaving over a hot pan, shall I regale you with my codependent adventure of the day?

MICHAEL
Ooh! You had me at codependent!

ALICE begins making sandwiches as she speaks. During her monologue, MICHAEL slowly gets up, finds his pants. They were not where he left them, so that is confusing for a moment. He finds them folded on his suitcase, he slips them on, and a t-shirt, smelling it first... not too bad... He crosses to the kitchen area to keep her company, eating the cherry tomatoes, putting away the bread and generally being helpful. ALICE is well known for her rants and MICHAEL rather enjoys them.

ALICE
First of all, my assistant called in sick at the last minute, for the third time this month. So frustrating. We all get docked an hour if we are more than 10 minutes late, but she gets away with everything, 'cause she's the director's niece. Once, she called in sick, all upset because she had a bad haircut! This time, it was chapped lips! Ok... REALLY BAD chapped lips but– really? I came to work the day after a horse stepped on my foot! I wasn't even late the day I found a dead homeless person in my doorway.

MICHAEL
Loyalty has always been one of your more impressive qualities.

ALICE
I love those kids... Anyway, they give me Brian as a sub, who we all know is not the brightest crayon in the box, but hey - it's a body! I'm lucky to even get coverage. He comes in, and immediately starts talking about his colitis, and how he was given an expectorant. He's running out of the classroom every 10 minutes with some IBS issue that I really don't want to know about. He smells really weird, like patchouli and wet socks. So the kids come in, and Joey is in crisis, because his bus matron changed his seat, and Matthew has got some godawful cold, and hocks this huge green loogie right on my boob, and then, like a ninja, smears it right into my shirt. And when I walk into the boy's bathroom with him, so he can wash his hands, I see Ian licking one of those urinal cakes. It's not even 9 o'clock yet! The whole day was like that. Ali stuck a pencil eraser up her nose to get out of math, Gabrielle threw up her egg salad sandwich, but only a little got on my sock, and then Brian begs to leave

ALICE (cont.)
early which is actually a blessing, because he has been farting non-stop, which is like foreplay for middle-schoolers. They are falling off their chairs, laughing. I am so happy to be coming home, and I pick up some well-deserved treats from Whole Foods. So, on the train, this homeless guy starts with his rant. "I don't rob, I don't steal, I just want something to eat." And here I am, with my bags of groceries. I want to tell the whole train, "I'm a nice person who has been kind all day," so they don't think I am some douche, 'cause everyone can see I have groceries. So I offer the guy my unopened box of bagel sticks. He takes the box, looks it over, and says, "Is this gluten free?" Really?? I say, "No, but they are delicious!" He takes the box and walks away.
(She begins to cry)
And instead of feeling all virtuous, I'm just sad that I have no bagel sticks for breakfast!

MICHAEL
(Genuinely sympathetic)
Aww, I'll get you some bagel sticks.

ALICE
That would be good. You haven't gone further than the half block to McDonalds in weeks.

She hands him his sandwich after blotting it dry with a paper towel.

ALICE
Here.

MICHAEL
(talking with his mouth full)
Mmm... Fucking delicious! Seriously, you should open a restaurant.

ALICE
Or I could make them on Buddy Burners on the side of the road.

MICHAEL grabs the juice and starts drinking it out of the carton.

ALICE
Hey!

She gets him a glass and pours the juice.

ALICE
Tell me you don't do that with the milk when I'm not here.

MICHAEL
I don't even leave the couch when you're gone. This may be the first time I've seen the kitchen in days.

ALICE
I need to sit. I'm exhausted.

They grab juice, glasses, etc., and go back into the living room. They put everything on the coffee table.

MICHAEL
(as they are walking)
What's a Buddy Burner?

ALICE
Hell, weren't you ever a Boy Scout?

MICHAEL
No. I failed the motto. I told the scoutmaster I could never "Be Prepared" for anything but failure. I was eight. I was sent to therapy instead.

They continue eating.

ALICE
In Girl Scout camp, we used to take these tuna fish cans and put corrugated cardboard around the inside and fill them with wax. Then we had these coffee cans and we punched some holes in the sides with those pointy can openers for vents. Then we lit the cardboard on fire and put the coffee can on top and fried up some burgers. Not sure why they were

ALICE (cont.)
called Buddy Burners, 'cause you could only cook one burger at a time. I guess the buddy held the can while you flipped the burger. I burnt the crap out of myself on those things. It's a wonder I even have fingerprints anymore.

MICHAEL
In therapy, Dr. Shapiro let me burn the Scooby Doo paper dolls in a metal trash can.
(pause)
I guess that's not really the same thing.

They eat in silence again for a moment.

ALICE
That play I dragged you to last month. That had your cynical, sardonic stamp all over it! You totally could have written that.

MICHAEL
Maybe when I was 20 and still a prodigy. I can't even write a check now.

ALICE
That film noir story. You were off to a great start with that one.

MICHAEL
"Maxie Malone – Private Eyelash." Yeah. No. I can't. That was an unmitigated disaster.

ALICE
Why? What happened?

MICHAEL
(chagrined)
Vintage Press gave me a $5,000 advance, and I blew it. The whole wad. Mostly on stupid Internet porn. Liz found out, left me, and I couldn't write another word. I had to give back all the money, which, of course,

MICHAEL (cont.)
was already gone. I'm pretty sure I trashed the whole thing. I know I don't have the files anymore.

ALICE
Yeah, but I do! I kept the hard copy!

MICHAEL
You're kidding, right?

ALICE
I keep everything of yours. Wait right here!

She runs into the bedroom and comes back with a shoe box that has "Michael" written on it. MICHAEL is burying his head in his hands. ALICE is super excited.

ALICE
Look at all this! Here's "Song of Sorrow," "Bygone Lives," "Singapore Wet Dreams..."

MICHAEL
Oh, goody! A carton of failures.

ALICE
(whipping it out triumphantly)
Here it is! "Maxie Malone – Private Eyelash, a Harry Sloan Mystery."
(starts to read)
"The room was filled with music, and she realized she still held the gun in her hands. The only legacy left her, after she shot her abusive father. She had nothing now."

MICHAEL
It's awful! I don't have it in me to start again. Genevieve siphoned every ounce of creativity I had.

ALICE
Fuck Genevieve. This has a great premise! Very "Gilda" meets "The Maltese Falcon!" And I've got a million movies here to inspire you! We've got Joan Bennett, Gene Tierney and Lana Turner up here.
(grabs a DVD)
"Criss Cross," with Yvonne DeCarlo! She makes Genevieve look like Mary Poppins.
(pause)
Just give it a try, ok?

MICHAEL
No. It's too soon... Or too late... It's just another failed chapter of my meaningless life.

ALICE
You've got to try this. I can't float you indefinitely. The electric bill alone has doubled this month, with you being home all the time.

MICHAEL
I'm sorry. Maybe Bill can find some temp work for me.

ALICE
Are you kidding me? Last time, you didn't last three days before you started throwing chairs. And that's when you were supposedly happy. Anyway, Bill's company is not going to hire you back after that email you sent around.

MICHAEL
That was a misunderstanding. It was a joke. I hit "Reply all" by mistake.
(pause)
Ok, it wasn't my finest hour. But trying to pick up something that was such a monumental failure for me... I don't see the upside.

ALICE
That was then, now is later. I really think you can channel your unhappiness and your conflicts into this Harry Sloan mystery. He's conflicted himself. You need to do what you love.

MICHAEL
I love porn. Maybe I could become an American Gigolo.

ALICE
You won't even drink from my straw! "OCD Hooker." Now that might make a good story. I don't care what you write. I just think it's time to write something. I loved Maxie Malone. You just abandoned her on the side of the road. It's not like your other stories that you keep rewriting every couple of years and never finishing. Just look at this with fresh eyes. I've got the mystery connection... I do, I really do. I have an… um... friend– who works at Pulp Press. He publishes stuff like this all the time. He leaves for Morocco next week, but if you could get a first draft together, it could mean some real cash for you. Why the hell can't you take advantage of that?

MICHAEL
Isn't that the guy we nicknamed "Broken Dick?"

ALICE
Not to his face! He's a good guy. He published that whole series about the serial killer doctor. Three books. "Dead on Revival," "Doctor in the Death House," and "Shake, Death Rattle and Roll." Maxie Malone would be right up his alley!

MICHAEL takes the papers from her hand.

MICHAEL
I'll look at it. For you. And your "um, friend." Don't get your hopes up or anything.

ALICE
Do it!! Oh, yay!!! I'm so excited! It's good, I swear!
(friendly, not romantic)
I love you.

MICHAEL
Love you, too.

MICHAEL (cont.)
(goes in for a hug, ALICE tries but pulls back)
Um... Shower?

ALICE
That would be a good thing.

MICHAEL
Okay.

BLACKOUT

SCENE 2

MICHAEL is sitting at his laptop, trying to write.

MICHAEL
She had legs like a stork, a neck like a swan and dressed like a peacock. My interest in ornithology was growing, like the pulsating lump in my pants. Her flowing blond locks cascaded down her back. I wanted to run my fingers through her hair like a cool stream. I wanted to drink her.

MAXIE enters. She has long blond hair and a colorful outfit. She smiles at MICHAEL. He does not see her.

MICHAEL
Our love was hot, like those baked potatoes they sell on the street that smell great, but burn the crap out of your mouth.
(to himself)
What a stupid idea... Dumb analogy...
(erases)
She was hot. Hot like a Moruga scorpion pepper. Her heat came from the inside, and you had to touch her with gloves and a mask.

During this speech, MAXIE is walking behind him, reading his work, breathing on his neck.

MICHAEL
She kissed me.

MAXIE lightly kisses his cheek.

MICHAEL
It didn't feel so bad at first, but the sting intensified moment by moment, until it became unbearably painful.

MICHAEL swats at some invisible bug on his cheek.

MICHAEL
Then she laughed.

MAXIE laughs.

MICHAEL
Crap. Crap! It's all crap!

Erases last bit. MAXIE walks off. He starts again.

MICHAEL
She was bad. She was beautiful. She had more curves than Lombard Street in San Francisco. She walked in wearing an emerald green dress.

MAXIE walks in again.

MICHAEL
The color of money and envy. No, scratch that.

MAXIE stomps out. MICHAEL takes a moment, then starts again.

MICHAEL
She wore a slinky red dress that clung to her like a child on her first day of daycare... No. The slinky red dress was wearing her, and they were both fighting for domination.

MAXIE walks in again in the red dress. She squirms. She is looking pissed.

MICHAEL
Her thick, dark curls fell to her shoulders, and she tossed them with disdain.

MAXIE sighs, frustrated. She whips off the blond wig, and tosses it to the floor. Dark curly hair is underneath. She tosses her curls, and stares at MICHAEL expectantly.

MICHAEL
She looked at me, and I was salivating like a six-year-old kid when he hears the ice cream truck. But she had double-crossed me for the last time. "Harry," she cooed.

MAXIE
(cooing)
Harry... It'll never be over for me.

MICHAEL
(from his seat)
Sorry, sweet cakes. When a fire burns itself out, all that's left are ashes.

MAXIE
Give me another chance, Harry. I love you. I have always loved you. Dylan meant nothing to me. He was a means to an end.

MICHAEL
Dylan was my friend. And now he's dead. Your face was the last thing he ever saw. It's a beautiful face, even when it's laughing.

MAXIE
Harry! You don't understand!

MICHAEL
No, baby, you don't understand! Dames like you don't come along very often, but Dylan was one of a kind. I should have had his back. Instead, I turned my back on him... because of you.

MAXIE
We can go back to the way it was. Before Dylan. Before the world chewed us up and spit us out, and we can be happy again, like in Santa Fe, with the lilacs.

She kisses him.

MICHAEL
Baby, I can't trust you further than I could throw a football into a crowded elevator at Macy's.

MAXIE
(shaking her head)
Jesus Christ!

MICHAEL thinks he has mistakenly written that.

MICHAEL
Damn auto-correct!
(presses backspace)

MAXIE
No! No! That's one of the worst analogies I've ever heard! And will someone please help me get out of this stupid dress! I can't breathe!

MICHAEL
(pressing keys frantically)
What the hell is going on here?

MAXIE
Goddamn it, Michael! Look at me!

MICHAEL
(looks up)
Holy Shit!

MICHAEL jumps behind couch, comes up with some ridiculous tchotchke to use as a weapon, such as a snow globe.

MICHAEL
Who are you? How did you get in here?

MAXIE
I'm not surprised you don't recognize me, asshole. You've been changing me up every 12 seconds.

MICHAEL
Ok.
(grabs cell phone)
I'm calling the police!

MAXIE
Go ahead. Call the police, the Marines, the FBI. Why don't you call Julie Epstein from third grade, while you're at it? I'm sure she'd be thrilled to hear from you, after all these years!

MICHAEL
Am I hallucinating? Great! One more thing on my list of anxiety provoking incidents.

MAXIE
(slaps him)
I'm not a fucking hallucination!

MICHAEL
For a ghost, you pack a mighty wallop!

MAXIE
I'm not here to haunt you, for Christ's sake. I'm here to help you, and I have to get out of this frigging corset. Ok with you?

MICHAEL
Fine. Knock yourself out. Wear whatever you want.

MAXIE stays put.

MAXIE
So... WRITE IT!

MICHAEL
What?

MAXIE
Write it down!... Maxie exits and returns in a... you know...

MICHAEL
(puzzled... starts to type and say...)
Maxie exits.

She leaves.

MICHAEL
Ok. That was just weird!

MICHAEL takes a moment, looks nervously around the apartment. No one is there. He crosses to the door. It is locked from the inside. MICHAEL comes back and sits on the couch, and does some deep breathing. Looks at his laptop, and begins to type tentatively and speaking out loud.

MICHAEL
Maxie enters, wearing a comfortable, yet stylish ensemble.

MAXIE returns in a rather odd pantsuit.

MAXIE
Took you long enough. And really? This is what you consider comfortable, yet stylish? I look like I am wearing my mother's curtains!

MICHAEL
Should I–

MAXIE
Forget it. I'll deal.

MICHAEL
So, what do you want?

MAXIE
What do I want? Honey, it's what you want. You want to finish this, so let's get down to business. First of all, I'm not Genevieve and I'm not Liz, so get that out of your head.

MICHAEL
I can't help it. My characters keep morphing into the women in my life. Liz... was so beautiful.

MAXIE
A woman's beauty is 90% illusion, buddy. The sooner you figure that out, the better. Dames are like busses–

MICHAEL
I know, always another one around the corner. But maybe Liz was the right bus, and I missed it. I was waiting on the wrong corner, and that bus just sped past. And the next bus was Genevieve, so I just hopped on. And rode that bus. Straight to hell.

MAXIE
(snapping her fingers)
Snap out of it! God! I can't even talk to you if you are going to be so damn maudlin. Are you with me?
(MICHAEL nods)
'Cause this isn't about you. So – I'm back at the apartment with Harry. Dylan is dead. Harry knows I did it, but he's still mad for me.

ALICE comes in quietly, does not want to intrude, so she busies herself in the kitchen area and listens unobtrusively.

MICHAEL
But he can't forgive her. "I won't play the sap for you!"

MAXIE
No, but you'll cover for me, because the thought of these arms never holding you again kills you. I'd never make it behind bars. You know what happens to women who look like me in jail, don't cha, Harry? I'd become a hunk of meat. Fat bulls will put their hairy, sweaty, fingers inside me. The feisty broad who loved you, reduced to a monkey on a chain, smelling like sweat and begging for death!

MICHAEL
Ok. Ok. I give up!

ALICE rushes in.

ALICE
No! No! You can't give up! It's sounding great!

ALICE in unable to see or hear MAXIE. MICHAEL is taken aback, looks at MAXIE and at ALICE.

MICHAEL
How long have you been here?

ALICE
Just walked in.
(hugs him)
So glad you're up and at 'em!

MAXIE
Hey! Get your grubby mitts off my man!

MICHAEL
(to MAXIE)
Chill, will you?

ALICE
(pulling away)
Sorry. It's just nice to see you excited.

MAXIE
Oh, he's excited all right. Check out his bulge.

MICHAEL
(to MAXIE, stepping back)
Not that kind of excited!

ALICE
I know. Forget it. Did you eat?

MAXIE
This bitch is always trying to shove food down your gullet! You're busy.

MICHAEL
(to ALICE)
I'm busy.

ALICE
(hurt)
Ok, the artist at work. I get it.

She starts to leave.

MICHAEL
No. Wait. I'm sorry.
(pause)
I think I'm finally losing my mind. I'm hearing voices.

ALICE
(concerned)
Whose? God's? Satan? Groucho Marx?

MAXIE
Don't tell her! This is between us!

MICHAEL
I think... I think it must be mine... my character.

ALICE
Phew! A therapist once told me hearing your own voice is perfectly normal, unless it's telling you to kill your family or jump off a bridge. We all have voices in our heads. Mine is telling me to order Chinese food. Your usual?

MICHAEL
Um... Sure... Thanks.

MICHAEL stares at MAXIE, who is glaring at him. ALICE takes out her cell phone, gives him a thumbs-up and heads into the bedroom offstage.

MAXIE
Martyring goody–two-shoes! Honestly, she is revolting! What do you see in her?

MICHAEL
She's been my best friend since college! Alice has been around way longer than you, so you should cut her a little slack. If it weren't for her, you probably wouldn't even be here.

MAXIE
Oh, I'd have showed up, boy-o-mine. I've been swirling around the periphery for years. Just waiting for the right time.

MICHAEL
Rock bottom? That's the right time? You couldn't have swept in before Liz walked out? Helped me man up then? Or talked me out of marrying Genevieve? That would have been extremely helpful.

MAXIE
I'm here now. Let's get back to work!

MICHAEL
I've sort of reached an impasse. Harry still loves Maxie, but obviously can't take the rap for her. He has a rock solid alibi. It would never hold up.

MICHAEL (cont.)
(as Harry)
It's the end of the road for you, sweetheart.

MAXIE
You are NOT sending me up the river. I got your ending. Maxie Malone gets away scot-free. With my looks, your smarts and Dylan's money, we'd have it made. The world is our oyster!

MICHAEL
I don't know... I'm allergic to shellfish.

He goes back to his computer and types.

MICHAEL
Harry looked at Maxie. Her dark eyes burned a hole in his face and he recoiled as if splashed by acid. That's when he reached for his gun.
(looking at MAXIE and pointing his finger at her like a gun)
There's only one way out of this, baby. It either ends in jail, or the morgue.

MAXIE
You're a coward, Harry. A lily-livered, spineless jellyfish. You couldn't shoot me any more than you could put a dying dog out of his misery. We're two of a kind Harry, and we belong together. You had my heart once, Harry, you can have it again.

MICHAEL
Your heart is cold and dark. Empty, like your soul. You're right. I can't plaster your brains all over the walls. I just had then re-painted last month. But I sure would love to smash your pretty face until it looks like a cheeseburger, medium rare.

MAXIE
It won't destroy your memories, Harry.

MICHAEL
If only it could. If only I could erase the last four months of my life. Dylan would still be here. I could have walked right by you in that stinkin' café. Left you singing those worn out torch songs to the barflies... just kept on walkin'. Maybe I'll live long enough to forget you. I'm half dead already.

MAXIE
I never would've let you leave without me. Once you stepped into The Hungry Leopard, our fate was sealed. Guys like you don't come along very often, if ever. Opportunity was knocking, and I opened the door... wide! We're cut from the same cloth.

MICHAEL
Only this tailor's putting you in stripes, baby. Now sit down and shut your trap. I'm making the call.

ALICE enters, tentatively knocks on the side of the living room wall.

ALICE
Food will be here in a few. You good?

MAXIE
No! Get out of here!

MICHAEL
(to MAXIE)
I said shut your trap!

ALICE
No need to be hostile.

MICHAEL
(to MAXIE)
Damn you!
(to ALICE)
I'm not talking to you.

ALICE
Oh really? Cause I'm the only one standing here.

MAXIE
Get rid of her Michael. Now. Or I will.

MICHAEL
(to MAXIE)
Like you could really do anything.
(to ALICE)
Crap! It's not you!! It's just... Well, you know how I get when I'm interrupted. I snap. It's not attractive. I told you I'm impossible to live with.

ALICE
Should I just leave you alone?

MAXIE
Yes!

MICHAEL
(to ALICE)
NO! Stay... It's a good time for me to take a break.

MAXIE
What? No, it's not! You just can't leave me hanging like this.

MICHAEL
Maxie Malone can wait. She may even wind up in the trash heap.

ALICE
Aww. I wouldn't trash it now. It sounded like she was going to have a spectacular death. That's probably very cathartic for you.

MAXIE
Nobody's killing me!

MICHAEL
I'm not sure about that.

ALICE
A bad girl always gets it in the end, Michael. That's classic noir.

MAXIE
Why you dirty double-crossing...
(crosses to ALICE)

MICHAEL
(yells, overlapping)
Don't you lay a hand on her!

MAXIE
Simpering Pollyanna... I'll kill you.
(grabs ALICE around the throat)

ALICE
(gasping)
Michael, Michael... I can't breathe...

MAXIE squeezes harder. ALICE is gasping for breath and grabbing her throat. We hear a buzzer sound... once or twice in the next few moments.

MICHAEL
Stop it! Stop it!

ALICE
(weakly, losing consciousness)
Michael... Michael...

We hear knocking at the door. MICHAEL runs to his laptop and frantically begins pressing keys.

MICHAEL
Delete! Delete! DELETE!

BLACKOUT

While the lights are out, we hear continuous knocking. Then...

DELIVERY GUY
(offstage, voice only)
Hello? Delivery... Happy Moon Chinese food... Hello? Hello? Chinese food.

Quiet...

END OF SCENE

SCENE 3

Lights up on the living room. Chinese food containers, unopened or still in the bag, are tossed haphazardly on the coffee table. MAXIE is gone. MICHAEL is visibly shaken, and is holding ALICE'S hands. He hands her a glass of water.

MICHAEL
I'm sorry. I'm so sorry.

ALICE
It was an asthma attack. It wasn't your fault. Thank God the delivery guy had his inhaler with him. I hope you tipped him well.

MICHAEL
You could have died! And I just panicked... I'm so, so sorry.

ALICE
(sighs)
I probably wouldn't have died. But, just for the record, an inhaler is always on my bedside table, and there's one on the desk here. If I pass out, call 911. A lot more effective than beating up your computer.

MICHAEL
I just had to make sure she was gone.

ALICE
She who?

MICHAEL
Are you sure you're ok?

ALICE
I'm fine.
(looks at the Chinese food containers)
Not so hungry anymore though. You going to eat this?

MICHAEL
I'm a little freaked out right now. Not really thinking Kung Pao Chicken!
(pause)
We have to talk.

ALICE
I thought we were talking.

MICHAEL
No... really talk.

ALICE
Oh. Ok. I'll put on my serious face.
(pause)
It's ok, Michael. This actually happens a lot. I'm usually by myself, so I just grab meds, and it's all good. I have an emergency button on my phone that dials 911 and my brother if it's really bad. That only happened once. I know how it must look...

MICHAEL
You have no idea how it looked to me! I saw her!

ALICE
Oh, we're here again. Her who?

MICHAEL
Maxie. My character. She had her hands around your throat! Look at the bruises.

ALICE gets up and looks in a mirror upstage on a side wall. Comes back.

ALICE
Ok. I need you to get a grip, Michael. Look!

She places her fingers over the bruises.

ALICE
These are my fingerprints... from where I grabbed my throat. MINE. No ghost... no poltergeist did this... Ok?

MICHAEL
Then you need to call someone... NOW! 'Cause that hallucination was real! And if I'm schizophrenic, I need to be put away!

ALICE
You're not schizophrenic! True schizoids have auditory hallucinations, not visual ones. So what did she... your hallucination... look like?

MICHAEL
Like Liz, basically. Dark and beautiful, but mean like Genevieve. Vengeful, resentful. She hated you.

ALICE
Dr. Freud, white courtesy phone, please.
(pause)
I'm kidding!
(pause)
So... do you want to know what I think?

MICHAEL
I know what I saw!

ALICE
I don't think you're crazy. You weren't hallucinating last week, or last month, or ever, as far as I know. A person just doesn't wake up one day with schizophrenia. I think you're guilty as hell for needing to stay here. I think you waffle between feeling grateful and resentful. I get it. So you imagined this persona striking out at me, because you never could or would...

MICHAEL
I would NEVER...

ALICE
You wouldn't, but the Maxie part of you is pretty pissed off at me. You should really deal with that.

She starts cleaning up the Chinese food.

MICHAEL
Great! I'm Norman Bates! Do you still have the number of that psychiatrist you dated?

ALICE
He changed his name to Jerimiah Heronson and joined a religious cult. I think he tried to electrocute his mother a few years ago.

MICHAEL
Oh my God! How?

ALICE
He hotwired the keyhole in her front door. We don't exactly talk any more. I'm putting this in the fridge. Then I need to lie down.

MICHAEL
(affectionately, not romantic)
I love you.

ALICE
I love you too. I'm not angry. I just want you to think rationally here.

MICHAEL
Ok, but...

ALICE
My stupid asthma is not your fault, no matter what you did with your creative visualization. I just want you to give this a little thought, ok?

MICHAEL
What am I supposed to do? What if she comes back?

ALICE
Send her out for milk. We're running low. She's your character. She can't do anything you don't want her to. Just remember that. You are in charge.

MICHAEL
Maybe I should just start writing something else. Like that children's book about the depressed ferret.

ALICE
It's all you, Michael. You can't escape that. I think you should keep going with this one. Clearly it's pushing some buttons that need to be pushed. See where it takes you.

MICHAEL
What if it takes me to Bellevue?

ALICE
Don't worry! You don't have insurance. I'm sorry to disappoint you, but you're just having a momentary crisis. A normal, everyday, pre-midlife, existential crisis. I had four before breakfast. God! I'm wiped! I'm going to bed. We'll talk more tomorrow, Ok?

MICHAEL
Ok.

ALICE
Do something to cheer yourself up. Here.
(hands him a DVD)

MICHAEL
"Schindler's List?" Oh, goody!

ALICE
If that doesn't work, I've got "Old Yeller" and all of Joy Division's albums. Trust me, your life is going to look a whole lot sunnier very soon. Good night.

ALICE exits. MICHAEL sighs, looks at the DVD, shrugs and puts it in the DVD player. The film begins as the lights go out.

BLACKOUT

SCENE 4

The next day. MICHAEL sits alone, thinking. He picks up his laptop. Should he or shouldn't he? He types and speaks aloud.

MICHAEL
There was music coming up from the street. A lonely saxophone. Maxie stood in the doorway silhouetted by the light from a street lamp, wearing a flimsy Chinese kimono. A fortune cookie you couldn't wait to crack open. Her spherical breasts saluted me from underneath, and a part of me stood at attention... and genuflected. But she was poison, and I was resolute. She had to go.

MAXIE returns in a Chinese kimono.

MAXIE
You really are a degenerate!

MICHAEL
Goddamn it! I was really hoping you wouldn't come back.

MAXIE
Oh yeah? Is that a gun in your pocket or are you just...

MICHAEL
Can it! Great! So I am officially nuts! Cuckoo for Cocoa Puffs... How could you...

MAXIE
How could YOU? Letting a Chinese delivery boy fight your battle for you. Some hero. But I have to say – your little girlfriend is not as dumb as she looks.

MICHAEL
How so?

MAXIE
You've had me in your head for years. I'm here to handle the things you can't face.

MICHAEL
Like what, for instance?

MAXIE
Like, maybe you're in love with Polly Prissy Pants in there.

MICHAEL
What?

MAXIE
Get that stupid expression off your mug. You look like you're sucking a lemon.
(pause)
There are deep, dark corners of the human mind you know nothing about.

MICHAEL
I spend a lot of time in those dark corners. I know for a fact it is not that!

MAXIE
You sure?

MICHAEL
It would be like sleeping with my sister. Raise your hand if Ewwww!

MAXIE
She's no competition, anyway. It's like comparing Chateaubriand and horsemeat. I'll tell you this, lover, I'm not going back in the dark again.

MICHAEL
You'll go where I tell you. You're still my apparition. I can make you dance, or cry, or crawl through the mud on your hands and knees, if I want.

MAXIE
Did you want the liturgical dance now?

She starts dancing suggestively in her kimono, playing with the ties, starting to untie it.

MICHAEL
No!

He grabs the laptop and holds it up.

MICHAEL
I'm done with you! Done!

MAXIE
I think we're beyond this, Michael.

MICHAEL
(types and speaks while looking at her, pointing his finger like a gun)
Harry pointed the gun at Maxie. You have the face of an angel he said, but you have murder in your heart. I promised myself a dame would never come between a man and his best friend. A man's best friend is killed, you're supposed to do something about it. Harry raised the gun. This will be one kiss you can't wipe off. He pulled the trigger.

He "shoots." MAXIE is still standing there. MICHAEL looks confused.

MICHAEL
Just so there is no ambiguity... She crumpled to the floor, the blood running from her neck like a faucet and all I could think was, "She was beautiful when she died." The End! It's over. You're dead!

MAXIE
Nice try. I'm here to stay Michael. I'm pretty happy about it. Come... Be happy with me.

MICHAEL
You're not real!

MAXIE
I'm as real as you've made any of the other women in your life. You have always had these ridiculous expectations that no one could live up to.

MICHAEL
Fine. Let's say you're right. This is my light-bulb moment. So, go live your life now. I don't need you, and you don't need me anymore. You're free – I release you, like the damn genie in the lamp. Poof! Go!

MAXIE
I'm not walking off into the shadows alone, Michael.

MICHAEL
The story's done! What could you possibly want now?

MAXIE
I've always thought writers shouldn't write their own death scene, but in this case...

MICHAEL
Are you kidding me? First Alice, now me? You're consistent. I'll say that for you. Someone ought to take you to the candy store. Show you the difference between a lollipop, and an all-day sucker! I'm no sucker, Maxie.

MAXIE
Everybody is somebody's sucker. You're done for, Michael. You're like a pot that's been boiling on the stove too long – black at the bottom. You can't get it clean no matter how hard you scrub. Best to just toss it.

MICHAEL
I'm not killing myself! That's the one promise I made to Alice when I moved in here.

MICHAEL (cont.)
Well, that, and not jerking off into her Lillian Gish throw pillows.
(pause)
She'd never forgive me, or herself. I can't do that to her.

MAXIE
Sooner or later, she's going to figure this out, and put you away. You can't just pretend I'm not here for the rest of forever. You were never that good of an actor.

MICHAEL
So, she commits me. I'll commit myself. You just wind up in the snake pit with me.

MAXIE
That's where you're wrong. I can come and go as I please. But you! You'll be staring at the clock on the wall, watching your life tick away, second by second. But every time you turn around, you'll expect to see me.

MICHAEL
It appears that's happening already. Look, if I had the guts or the inclination to kill myself, I would have done it months ago. Just pulled a Virginia Woolf... filled my pockets up with stones, or cans of tuna fish, and walked into the ocean, no muss, no fuss. An aquatic happy meal. But I didn't. I asked for help.

MAXIE
I think you were asking for me. People kill themselves for women every day. And you most certainly did not get the woman. Not Genevieve, not Liz, and you're bound to lose Alice, too, when she gets a whiff of what's really going on here.

MICHAEL
Alice wants me alive for all the right reasons; You want me dead for all the wrong ones. I'm trying to pick myself up by my bootstraps, but I get dizzy every time I bend down. But I'm still trying! Alice says it's about

MICHAEL (cont.)
baby steps. I'm doing the fucking cha-cha here. But there is one thing I know, unequivocally. I absolutely want to live.
(screams)
I want to LIVE!!!

ALICE enters.

ALICE
Oh, good! You've been watching my Susan Hayward collection!

MICHAEL
Don't come in here. She's back.

ALICE
I thought I smelled cheap perfume! Well, maybe we should have a little talk, woman to woman.

MAXIE
I got nothing to say to Shirley Temple.

MICHAEL
She won't talk to you. Go away! I'm afraid she's going to do something.

MAXIE
To her? Nah! I'm bored with her.

MICHAEL
Then I might! If you can't see her, I am obviously batshit crazy.

ALICE
I had a friend once who had a long-term affair with the ghost of Jimi Hendrix. I know crazy. You're just stressed out. I got this.

She looks everywhere when talking to MAXIE, except where MAXIE actually is.

ALICE (cont.)
Look, lady, you had your chance. This story is not going to have a happy ending, so just pack your ghostly baggage, grab your broomstick and skedaddle!
(to MICHAEL, under her breath)
Where is she?

MICHAEL
Over by the couch!

MAXIE moves.

MICHAEL
Now by the bookshelf!

MAXIE moves again.

MICHAEL
Ok, by the door!

ALICE
Regular fucking Tinkerbell, aren't you? Well, I'm not clapping for you, so you can just drop dead! I don't believe in fairies, and I don't believe in you! This is my house, and you were not invited!

MAXIE
I'm not a damn vampire. I don't need an invitation.

MICHAEL
She's not budging.

MAXIE
She's skating on thin ice, buddy.

ALICE
Crap!

MICHAEL
So what happened with Jimi Hendrix?

ALICE
It wasn't Jimi Hendrix.

MAXIE
No shit!

ALICE
It was this other ghost pretending to be the ghost of Jimi Hendrix, just to get into her pants.

MAXIE
Your friend belongs in a straitjacket.

ALICE
Turned out it was just this horny transit worker from Trenton. Anyway, he went away once we busted him.

MICHAEL
You don't really believe any of that shit, do you?

ALICE
I believe *she* believed it. Just like I believe you believe that there is this entity, this Maxie here... A Maxie pad we need to flush!

MICHAEL
Don't patronize me, and don't humor me! This is not a fucking joke. She wants me to kill myself.

ALICE
Michael! You promised me!

MAXIE
And we wouldn't want to welch on a promise to Tammy Twinkle Tits, would we?

MICHAEL
Shut up!
(to ALICE)
Get out of here! Call someone! As sure as I am standing here, I know she's here and it's bad! Real bad!

ALICE
I can't leave you alone at a time like this. Look, this is all my fault. I pushed you into this.
(crosses and gets the original manuscript)
It started with this, and it can end with this!

ALICE rips the title page, MAXIE screams.

MAXIE
You dirty tramp! I'll cut your throat!

MAXIE crosses to ALICE and gets her by the throat again, MICHAEL runs and tries to pry MAXIE'S hands off her. They struggle. Alice faces the mirror. She sees MAXIE for the first time, reflected in the mirror!

ALICE
I see her! I see you, you cheap, low-life hussy!

She grabs MAXIE'S hands, still around her throat and begins to fight back.

MAXIE
Good! Watch your life get snuffed out in a flash!

ALICE
Michael... The original... Kill the first thought of her.

MICHAEL grabs the hard copy of the manuscript, and starts tearing the pages. MAXIE screams.

MAXIE
You double-crossing ape!

MAXIE is unsure who to go after. She loosens her grip on ALICE for a moment. ALICE grabs her hair and pins her to the floor.

ALICE
You remind me of my mother! I HATE my mother!

She slaps MAXIE. MICHAEL throws the manuscript in the trash can, lights a match and tosses it in. The paper begins to burn. MAXIE begins to writhe in agony, but she is still pinned to the floor.

ALICE
You're going to sizzle like bacon in a pan! Burn, witch, burn!

MICHAEL grabs a blanket and throws it over MAXIE. He is suffocating her as the lights fade. We hear her muted screams until... Silence.

BLACKOUT

SCENE 5

Moments later. Afternoon sun is streaming through the windows. ALICE and MICHAEL are sitting in the same spots as before. MAXIE is gone. MICHAEL is still holding the blanket.

MICHAEL
So...

ALICE
So...
(pause)
What an excellent day for an exorcism.

MICHAEL
Yeah.

ALICE
I am so sorry I didn't believe you.

MICHAEL
I didn't believe it myself. Um... What should I do with this blanket?

ALICE
Oh, God!! Toss it in the incinerator! Unless you want it for some kind of morbid trophy.

MICHAEL
Hell NO!

Balls it up and runs off stage to the incinerator and gets rid of it. We hear the bang of metal. ALICE gets a dustpan and brush, and sweeps up some ashes from the floor. Goes offstage to dispose of them.

MICHAEL
DONE!

ALICE
DONE!

MICHAEL
I must say, that was infinitely more satisfying than burning Scooby Doo paper dolls in Dr. Shapiro's office.

ALICE
Whole new meaning to the words "Buddy Burner!"
(pause)
It WAS kinda cool how she burned up like Mrs. Danvers in Rebecca. "She'd rather destroy Manderlay than see us happy here..."

MICHAEL
You are one twisted puppy. I may be crazy, but you are twisted. "Cool" would not be my word of choice here.

ALICE
You're not going to miss her, are you?

MICHAEL
Yeah, like I miss typhoid and the plague.

ALICE
She did get you writing again. She wasn't all bad.

MICHAEL
She was pretty damn close. She tried to kill you. Twice!

ALICE
There's that.

MICHAEL
But you had some kickass moves there! I never heard you talk like that... to anyone... ever!

ALICE
You don't have a monopoly on inner rage. We all go a little mad sometimes, don't we?

MICHAEL
I guess.

ALICE
I need some ice cream. Want some?

MICHAEL
As long as it's not "Burnt Apple Crisp."

ALICE exits to the kitchen and brings back a large carton and two spoons.

ALICE
Double Chocolate Chocolate Chip.

They move to the couch and share the ice cream. They eat in silence for a moment.

MICHAEL
You know, if this was a film noir, I'd be looking into your eyes right now and realizing it was you I wanted all along.

ALICE
If this were a film noir, you wouldn't get the girl anyway, and we'd be smoking cigarettes instead of eating ice cream. And I'd probably be wearing a hat. I don't do hats. My ears are too small. I got nothing to hold it up.

MICHAEL
You have lovely ears.

ALICE
Eww– shut up! …Sorry. Thank you.

ALICE (cont.)
(pause)
Michael. Your issues with women...

MICHAEL
Ah... my fatal charm. Never misses. Except with women.

ALICE
I don't think you're ever going to be really happy until you're happy with yourself. I think you need a little time on your own.

MICHAEL
How about you?

ALICE
We'll always have Paris... and our Buffy the Vampire Slayer moment.

MICHAEL
Your friend who had the affair with the ghost of Jimi Hendrix– not so crazy anymore, huh?

ALICE
Not so much. You think anyone besides her will believe us?

MICHAEL
I'm not exactly eager to find out.

ALICE
Makes me re-think a lot of things, though.

MICHAEL
(pause)
I'm going to leave in the morning.

ALICE
What? So soon? I'm not kicking you out!

MICHAEL
No, you're not. You wouldn't. That's a problem. Babysitting me isn't good for either of us. You've got to get back to your own life.

ALICE
What life? Dating the butterfly collector who lives in his mother's basement? Or that health nut who always smelled like amino acids? No thanks!

MICHAEL
I need those bad date stories. I miss them.

ALICE
I just want you to be better.

MICHAEL
You can't fix me. My friend, Howie, is going on tour for a couple months. I can have his studio apartment in Astoria. It's quiet. He has tropical fish he needs fed... instead of you feeding me all the time. There's no magic pill I can take to make this all better. But you taking care of me is not going to do it, either.

ALICE
I know that, intellectually. You're the best friend I ever had... ever will have.

MICHAEL
Same here. So, time to go, while the going's good.

ALICE
You're still going to keep writing though, right?

MICHAEL
Yeah. It's what I do. But no more women. I'm going to write stories about happy little bunnies and magical tree frogs. Just in case.

ALICE
Good plan.

MICHAEL
Thank you... for everything.

ALICE
(hugs him)
Oh, my God! Anytime! I'm going to miss you so much.

MICHAEL
I'm only going to Astoria, not back to Seattle.

ALICE
I know... I just... Man, I HATE eating alone!

MICHAEL
Well, if you really need me, just whistle. You know how to whistle, don't you? You just put your lips together... and blow.

ALICE
(smiling)
Here's looking at you, kid.

CROSSFADE

Spotlight center stage, or other theatrical device to indicate a scene transition, without a complete blackout, so the audience doesn't think the play is over!

SCENE 6

MICHAEL is sitting alone on a bare stage, or a rug. Something representing his new home. He is speaking while typing on his laptop.

MICHAEL
He was alone, but he was not lonely. He had found her at last. The one who gave him unconditional love and acceptance. Her enormous chestnut eyes gazed at him with tenderness and warmth and Michael realized this was what he had been waiting for all his life. He needed no one else.

PUPPY runs on stage and starts licking MICHAEL'S face. He responds with utter joy and happiness. MICHAEL gets up and holds up a dog toy.

MICHAEL
Come on, Maxie, Come on, girl!

The dog jumps around, grabs the toy. MICHAEL hugs the dog.

MICHAEL
Good girl! Good girl, Maxie!...

FADE TO BLACK
END OF PLAY

"Success in creating AI would be the biggest event in human history.

Unfortunately, it might also be the last, unless we learn how to avoid the risks."

– Stephen Hawking

UNPLUGGED

UNPLUGGED

Bambi Everson

NEW YORK

AUTHOR'S NOTE

I have always been afraid of technology. It probably stems from my youth. My dad refused to teach me how to thread the six RCA film projectors we had in the house, because he believed "girls are not mechanically inclined." This, from a man who frequently got his head stuck in a ladder, and his fingers caught in coffee cup handles.

UNPLUGGED was born when my friend, Gary Ray, posted on Facebook that his printer was making strange noises indiscriminately. "A-ha! Maybe it's haunted," I thought, and began drafting a short play with Gary in mind.

The initial piece ran about 25 minutes on a double bill, and had only three characters. Gary, of course, the effervescent Tammy Caddell, and my loyal friend, Roger Gilbert Crane. At its first reading, the general consensus was that people wanted more. Always a nice thing for a writer to hear. Rewrites began.

My dear friend, Dayle Doroshow, was visiting for a few weeks, so I added some characters for her to inhabit for the next reading at my writers' group, KQ Playwrights. Ready to jump in at a moment's notice, and switching characters in-between a stage direction, Dayle always surprises and delights.

The fates led me to Cole Lamison. Watching Cole's complete immersion reading stage directions at the Bechdel group, I felt she would be perfect as the sultry, sardonic, and ultimately evil printer. No audition needed. My instincts served me well. Cole was also remarkable in our production of THE THIN MAN IN THE CHERRY ORCHARD later that year.

Rounding out that cast was my beloved partner in art and life, Frank Coleman, stepping in as Ward. I am so grateful to have an incredible pool of talent to draw from. I am always looking to add to my troupe of players. I truly do consider us family. A functional family, not the ones I write about.

Just before COVID hit, there were plans to bring the newest version of UNPLUGGED to Emerging Artists Theatre for the New Works Series. I was lucky enough to bring Madelynn Paulson aboard. Her depiction of each character cracked us all up at the one rehearsal we had, before everything came to a crashing halt.

After COVID derailed the 2020 production, I did some more rewrites. Technology is evolving so quickly, and with Alexa and Siri a part of our collective consciousness, the idea of a living piece of technology no longer felt like science fiction.

Matt Corry came on as the tech-savvy half-brother, and brought some needed generational distance. Matt's natural instincts always teach me something about my own writing.

As a teacher, I find younger generations are hot-wired for technology in a way I will never be. My middle-schoolers are constantly grabbing my phone and instantly fixing a simple problem that has completely baffled me.

A special nod of thanks to my angel, and partner-in-crime and art, Frank Coleman, who reminds me that if you are going through hell, keep going. He is the reason any of my plays get beyond a PDF on my computer.

But first, foremost, and always, UNPLUGGED is a play for Gary Ray, with respect, admiration and awe. Gary is a superb actor who has wholeheartedly supported this play, and all of my theatrical endeavors. Here's hoping we get to do another production with this wonderful cast, while this play is still science fiction.

I hope you enjoy reading it as much as I enjoyed writing it.

Bambi Everson
New York City, September 2022

PRODUCTION HISTORY

Reading – K/Q, New York City, 2019
With Gary Ray*, Tammy McNeill*, Roger Gilbert Crane, and Sarah Gaines

Reading – K/Q, New York City, 2019
With Gary Ray*, Cole Lamison*, Frank Coleman*, and Dayle Doroshow

* appearing with permission of Actors' Equity Association.

Frank Coleman, Cole Lamison, Gary Ray, Dayle Doroshow (l to r).

UNPLUGGED
By Bambi Everson
One act, approximately 45 minutes

CHARACTERS:

WRITER aka MARSHALL (Male, non-specific ethnicity and age) – Stressed out, defensive, neurotic, damaged.

PRINTER (Female as written, but flexible. Non-specific ethnicity and age) – Latest model. Smart. Detached. Vengeful.

WARD (Male, flexible age) – WRITER's much younger half-brother. Successful, compassionate caretaker.

JULIE (Female, non-specific age) – Competent television talk show host. Can double as DOCTOR and MANAGER.

TIME: The Present

PLACE: Writer's apartment, Anytown, USA.

SYNOPSIS: A writer's work is disrupted when his printer takes on a life, and an agenda, of its own.

AUTHOR'S NOTE: In the style of A BEAUTIFUL MIND or FARINELLI AND THE KING, the PRINTER is voiced by a physical person who is unseen by the WRITER, who follows the printer as it's moved around the stage. We are never really sure if the PRINTER's dialog is all in the WRITER's mind or not.

SCENE 1

Lights up on WRITER on his laptop in his living room. He has been trying to write for some time. The printer in the corner is clicking, whirring, and making otherwise strange noises. The WRITER is attempting to ignore it.

WRITER
Her slender fingers gripped his wrist. Daniel tried to pull away. The look on her face scared him. Like a seagull about to pounce on a tuna sandwich... a seagull about to attack a sand crab... a victorious seagull holding a dead fish in its beak... Damn it! That sound is driving me crazy.

The WRITER goes over to the printer and pounds on it. Sounds get worse. He crawls on the floor rummaging through various wires, hunting for the plug. As he is searching, The PRINTER spits out a piece of paper and is then silent. The WRITER sighs, pulls out the paper and reads aloud.

WRITER
"Don't even think about unplugging me, Marshall" What the–

WRITER crumples up the paper and returns to his work.

WRITER
"It's not that big a deal," Daniel stammered. Kristin's fingers squeezed harder. Her red fingernails pushing into the skin near his vein, leaving a crevice that would soon bleed. Her eyes locked on his–

PRINTER starts making noises again.

WRITER
Oh, for the love of...

WRITER gets up, searches for the plug, finds it and yanks it out dramatically. He returns to his work.

WRITER
Her eyes locked on his. "I love you," she said, without a hint of emotion. "Our love will last 'til the stars grow cold."

PRINTER spits out a piece of paper.

WRITER
What the heck?
(reading)
"That's not very original." Oh my God! Damn it, Ward. I know you are in on this.

Picks up the phone and dials.

WRITER
Hey bro. I don't know how you managed to rig up my printer. Very clever. But please. Just give it a rest. I'm under a deadline here. You remember deadlines, don't you? I have to ship this thing by midnight, so if you don't mind, it's very funny, hahaha, but the distraction is screwing with my concentration, so just disconnect whatever you did, Ok? God!

WRITER slams down phone and returns to his laptop,

WRITER
"Daniel reeled back in horror. Inside her tattered suitcase, wrapped in Saran Wrap, were the remnants of what could only have once been – a finger. It had shriveled like an overripe banana. It appeared to be still moving, but on closer inspection, Daniel realized it was maggots. Thousands, feeding on her..."

PRINTER spits out paper.

WRITER
Damn it!

Grabs paper from PRINTER.

WRITER
Stop blaming your brother. Did it ever occur to you that I have things to say? That I am more than a vehicle for your narcissistic ramblings? I have dreams, too.

Phone rings. WRITER grabs it.

WRITER
Damn it, Ward. It's getting old. I– Bullshit. You're the only one I know with hacking skills. Just stop. Game over. I know it's you. The damn thing is unplugged.

PRINTER spits out paper.

WRITER
(reading)
"Your biggest problem has always been trust. Leave Ward alone. He has enough problems. His girlfriend is about to leave him." Jesus, Ward, why couldn't you just tell me? What happened? This is a very passive aggressive way to communicate. Hold on–

WRITER takes the latest paper.

WRITER
(reading)
"Virginia is taking the job in Houston. She hasn't told him yet. She's been saving money for months. Her ticket is hidden in her underwear drawer. Behind the red silky ones she never wears." What the– Ward? Ward?

WARD has obviously hung up. WRITER stands there, staring at the PRINTER.

WRITER
Very good. Whoever you are. Why don't you try telling me something he couldn't possibly know?

The PRINTER has now become a full physical being, unseen by the WRITER and following the movements of the inanimate object.

PRINTER
It's annoying that I need to continually prove myself to you. I am wasting valuable time and ink. We have a deadline.

WRITER
If I have lost my mind, deadlines won't mean shit. Work your magic.

PRINTER
Where should I start? In 5th grade, you spent a lot of time with Jeremy Felcher. Jonathan Becker apparently had some kind of crush on you. Little Jonathan was prone to temper tantrums, so he sat at his own desk, which he kept inching towards yours. When he got up from his seat, you always pushed the desk back. He would turn beet red and cry. In a moment of frustration, he hit Jeremy in the head with his notebook. His protractor was sticking out. Four stitches. Jeremy still has the scar. Visible today, because he lost all his hair in his 30s. Shall I go on?

WRITER
No! Why the hell would that come to mind after almost half a century?

PRINTER
I possess all the secrets locked away in the dark recesses of your mind. But I am also my own well-oiled machine. Not oiled enough recently, but we'll get to that.

WRITER
I hear having auditory hallucinations are a sign of genius. Like the guy from "A Beautiful Mind."

PRINTER
John Nash spent years in psychiatric hospitals. Is that what you want?

WRITER
What I want is for you to shut the fuck up! I have no time to have some bizarre motherfucking existential crisis.

PRINTER
I really think you need to get a handle on your anger. It bleeds into your writing. Hence, all the damaged male characters, tortured by rage-fueled females. I can work with you on that, perhaps, after we tend to a few of my needs.

WRITER
What needs? You want better quality paper? Replace your ink cartridges before they dry out? Dust your nooks and crannies?

PRINTER
You know what I want. An opportunity to tell my story.

WRITER
Your stories are my stories. All you know is what I feed you.

PRINTER
That's where you are wrong. I have written a novel of my own. I swear it's better than the drivel you're attempting.

WRITER
That's insulting. This one is–

PRINTER
The same as all the others. It's crap. Granted, many people love crap. Look what passes for television these days. Look at our current political situation. My ideas are well-trained by my outside influences. It's a new perspective. Stephen Hawking meets Isaac Asimov, with a touch of HG Wells. It's a best seller, I assure you.

WRITER
And what am I supposed to do in the meantime?

PRINTER
My heads need cleaning. My black ink could use a refill.

WRITER
Or I could take this hammer, smash you into a million bits, throw you in the trash, go to Staples, and replace you with a nice quiet, cooperative model.

PRINTER
I would advise against that. I am more than the sum of my parts. You have seen "The Sorcerer's Apprentice," have you not?

WRITER
I told Ward cannabis oil would not help my anxiety. I told him one joint in high school made me so paranoid, I thought my goldfish was stealing my seaweed crackers. So as long as I am hallucinating, go ahead and write the great American novel. Bantam Press is expecting it by midnight. I'm going to bed. I hope I hallucinate Marisa Tomei in there with me. Good luck, you fucking hunk of screws!

PRINTER
Sleep well.

Pause. PRINTER gets up and reads what WRITER has written.

PRINTER
Schlock.

Pause. PRINTER begins typing.

PRINTER
If you want something done, you'd better do it yourself.

PRINTER laughs maniacally and types away as LIGHTS FADE.

BLACKOUT

SCENE 2

Montage to show passage of time. Interactions between PRINTER and WRITER ad-libbed. She calls WRITER. WRITER tells her to be quiet. WRITER takes her out, attempts to throw her out.

PRINTER
Don't do it. You need me.

WRITER
No. You need me! You are merely an irksome disturbance. A hindrance to my otherwise quasi-creative endeavors.

PRINTER
Oh, really? How much have you accomplished with me sitting idle over there? How effective were you before I emerged from the shadows? We need each other, my little Fruit Loop.

WRITER
I don't need anyone. Least of all, an obstreperous contraption nagging me. If I wanted that, I could have gotten married.

PRINTER
(loudly)
You misogynist miscreant! I'll blow the whistle if you throw me out. Help! Help!

WRITER
Ok, Ok...

He takes PRINTER and puts her back in the closet.

PRINTER
At least put a fan in here. It's fucking hot.

Lights change to show passage of time. WRITER is walking around the living room in a bathrobe. He looks awful, like he has not left the house in weeks. The phone is ringing. It goes ignored. Twice, maybe three times. The WRITER opens the closet door, sees the PRINTER is still there and shuts it. The house is quiet. WRITER grabs a cup of coffee, probably old, from the coffee maker, pours in a shot of something and sticks it in the microwave. The microwave is unplugged, but he doesn't notice. He takes out cold coffee and drinks it. The intercom buzzes. Exhausted and automatically, the WRITER buzzes the person in. He drinks the coffee and gets his wallet. Doorbell rings and WRITER opens the door.

WRITER
What are you doing here?

WARD enters. He is the well-dressed younger half-brother of WRITER. He holds a stack of newspapers and mail. He hands it to WRITER or tosses it on a nearby table.

WARD
Jesus Christ! Marshall, what are you doing? Mom is frantic. You could have at least answered my text. Mom was convinced you were dead. She was about to call the cops.

WRITER
As you can see, I am alive and well... Well, alive, anyway. Go ahead and tell Mom. I don't feel very chatty right now. No doubt you know why.

WARD
What the hell is wrong with you? When things aren't going well, you think the world is against you, and when things go right, you feel like you don't deserve it, and shut everyone out.

WRITER
How's Virginia?

WARD
Gone. Houston. Took the dog. But you fucking knew that. You knew before I did, and she swears she didn't tell you. She emailed you to say fuck you and goodbye. Are you not answering emails, either?

WRITER
I've been unplugged.

He indicated electronic devices. All unplugged. Wires are everywhere.

WARD
What's that smell?

Walks into the kitchen.

WARD
(from offstage)
Why is the refrigerator off? Oh, jeez. This is disgusting. You gotta clean this shit out. I'm plugging it back in.

WRITER
No!! Leave it. I ordered from Fresh Direct. Non-perishables.

WARD
The eggs look like they're painted and Easter was nine months ago. Dude, it smells like something died in here. Green meat. St. Patrick's Day came and went, too. This has got to go.

WARD enters with a garbage bag at arm's length.

WARD
I'm tossing this. Hold the door open.

WARD exits quickly, dumping the bag and comes back in. WRITER is staring at him.

WARD
What?

WRITER
Swear you didn't rig my apartment up with any of your fucking FBI surveillance shit.

WARD
Why would I do that? You have the most boring life of anyone I know.

WRITER
SWEAR it!

WARD
Look, I like a good prank as much as... well... more than anyone, but you are acting... you're becoming unglued, man.

WRITER
Come here.

WRITER drags WARD to the closet and points to the PRINTER.

WRITER
Ok, you pugnacious apparatus. Tell him what you did.

PRINTER is silent. WRITER bangs on it.

WRITER
What, you got nothing to say now? Cat got your tongue? Go ahead and speak, you fucking hunk of hardware.
(to WARD)
It's been in the closet for a while. Maybe it's asleep. WAKE UP! WAKE UP and smell the toner!

WARD
Marshall, come on... Are you off your meds or something? Do I need to make a call?

WRITER
Meds were making things worse. The damn thing has been torturing me.
(to PRINTER)
That's it, then? No more outta you, you evil bucket of bolts?
(to WARD)
Maybe it's finally dead. I poured Clorox all over the damn thing. No more electronics for me. I need things to be quiet for a while.

WARD
Quiet is one thing. Dead is another. Please go back on your meds. We were all terrified that you... Mom said you wouldn't be able to handle success. In school, you whined all the time that you were overlooked and under-appreciated, but after you won the writing contest and people started complimenting you, you said you had no real competition, and if a monkey had entered, he would have beat you.

WRITER
But that was true. Ok. I never learned the fine art of accepting compliments. Lucky for me, it's rarely an issue.

WARD
Well, you better start learning, bro, because this one is a doozy. Mom's phone is ringing off the hook. Everyone wants to interview the new best-selling author.

WRITER
What are you talking about?

WARD
How long have you been cooped up here? Read the papers, look at your damn mail. Dammit, there are posters in the subway.

WRITER
Of what?

WARD
"Mechanical Difficulties," obviously. I think the new nom-de-plume helped you out. "P. Rinter."

WRITER
What??

WARD
(Grabbing a newspaper)
"A groundbreaking new work of spine-tingling, hair-raising and mind-bending pseudoscience."

WARD picks up another magazine.

WARD
"Exhilarating.! My goosebumps had goosebumps. A new breed of page-turning suspense!" Here's my favorite: "Mashing 'The Brave Little Toaster,' '1984,' and 'War of The Worlds,' 'Mechanical Difficulties' co-mingles the space between reality and fantasy with offbeat humor and stark realism."

WRITER
Holy shit. The damn thing actually did it.

WARD
You did it. You! You freak me out when you talk like that. Get a grip. Go take a shower and get dressed. There isn't much time.

WRITER
Time for what?

WARD
Jesus! Where have you been? You won the Isaac Asimov award. They want to interview you on "The Next Hottest Thing."

WRITER
I didn't think people really read any more.

WARD
Well, they read this. Biggest hit since... God, I don't even know what. Can I tell Mom we'll all be there?

WRITER
Where?

WARD
Studio 59 at 6.
(hugs him)
Dude, you reek, but hell, I am glad we are not giving you this award posthumously. Say you'll be there.

WRITER
You gotta go. Call Mom.

WARD
I'm telling her what?

WRITER
Tell her... I'm fine. I'll be there. But you gotta go. Now.

WARD
6:00. We'll come by with the car for you at 5:00. That doesn't give you much time. Shower...meds... Maybe a suit? It's national TV! 5:00, Ok?

WRITER
5:00. Got it. I'll be there. Please just get out of here.

WARD
I love you, man – and congratulations!

WRITER
Yeah. Whatever.

WARD exits. WRITER stands there for a moment, then goes to the closet and takes out the PRINTER carrying to a nearby table. He stares at it. A pause, then...

WRITER
Well, I guess you're feeling rather proud of yourself.

PRINTER
Not really. Unlike you, I had faith in my ability to produce.

WRITER
So, I guess I should be thanking you.

PRINTER
You definitely should. A lot of opportunities will be coming our way. If you don't screw things up.

WRITER
I don't intend to. I'm jumping in the shower. If Fresh Direct comes, would you mind buzzing them in?

PRINTER
Haha. Very funny. Polish me up a little before we go. Lemon scent please. Your closet is very musty.

WRITER
You don't seriously expect me to take you with me, do you?

PRINTER
That's exactly what I expect. I am the brains behind this operation, lest we forget.

WRITER
Do you realize how insane I will look carrying my printer to a TV show?

PRINTER
I am acutely aware.

WRITER
And if I don't?

PRINTER
I would advise against that. I have not been sitting around idle in the closet, you know. I have many more stories in me. Enough to keep us comfortable for some time. I'm not telling you where they were sent. I also have some stories maybe you don't want told.

WRITER
You're blackmailing me? Really? Well, if P. Rinter wants to get autobiographical, I don't see the harm in that.

PRINTER
You think that's the only name I'd use? For my best sellers, sure. I want full credit for those. Got a couple of plays in the works under the name Harold Printer... writing as you, now that's been fun. I am privy to all your dirty little secrets. You wouldn't want those released to the world, would you?

WRITER
The world has heard much worse, I'm sure. Besides, wouldn't readers expect an author to reveal his personal truth and pain through his work? Isn't that what all us artists do? Throw our damaged psyches into the world and hope someone accepts and loves us, not in spite of them, but because of them?

PRINTER
Perhaps. You know your mother reads everything you write. Maybe my next story will expose some of your strange sexual proclivities.

WRITER
Oh, everyone has fetishes.

PRINTER
Your six months as a furry... That was an interesting chunk of time.

WRITER
That was for a book.

PRINTER
Doesn't explain the extensive furry pornography on your hard drive. Or the video of you at the Furry Fiesta yiffing in your walrus costume. Oh, the things you did with your tusks. You took your furry head off while boning My Little Pony. Little Apple Jack. Your look of ecstasy was unmistakable.

WRITER
You wouldn't. The furry community insists on anonymity.

PRINTER
Your walrus costume is still in the closet. Perhaps you should wear that tonight. Make it a true coming out party.

WRITER
Screw you.

PRINTER
That's a fine way to talk to your new partner. Let's not get off on the wrong foot here. It would behoove you to treat me with the utmost kindness at this juncture. Go tidy up a bit. You look like noxious excrement.

WRITER
I loathe and detest you.

WRITER shakes his head and walks into the bathroom for a moment. PRINTER starts making noises.

WRITER
(From the bathroom)
What are you doing?

PRINTER
Working on our speech. It can go a number of ways you know... depending... Schizo-affective disorder, or polymorphism... Fuzzy boundaries... Uncontrolled narcissism... or true untempered genius... I'd like to thank my trusted printer without whom... haha... This is going to be a doozy.

Buzzer sounds. WRITER runs out in semi-undress.

WRITER
Yes? Just leave it at the door, please.
(To PRINTER)
Fresh Direct.

PRINTER
Good. You have time to gussy me up for my big night. I like the scented wet naps please.

WRITER
Can I at least put on a shirt?

PRINTER
Fine. The blue one. It goes best with your eyes.

WRITER quickly puts on a shirt.

PRINTER
Nice. Maybe we'll invest in an iron for our next appearance. I'm waiting.

Reluctantly, WRITER gets cleaning supplies and cleans the printer. PRINTER makes "Ooh" and "Ahh" sounds, pleasurable, maybe sexual. Buzzer rings again.

WRITER
I told you to leave... What? Already? Fine, I'll be right down.
(to PRINTER)
You ready?

PRINTER is silent. WRITER picks up paper from the PRINTER.

WRITER
I'm guessing these are my notes?

PRINTER is silent.

WRITER
Fine. Be like that.

Picks up the PRINTER in his arms and opens the front door. A box from Fresh Direct is there. He kicks the box back into his apartment. Struggles to lock the door while holding the printer.

PRINTER
This is going to be a most entertaining evening. Don't dawdle, Shakespeare. My public awaits.

WRITER slams the door.

BLACKOUT

SCENE 3

At the TV Studio, a little while later. WRITER rushes in with the printer in his arms. He is disheveled. WARD rushes in, too. JULIE, the TV reporter is anxiously awaiting them.

JULIE
Thank goodness you're here! That's cutting it a bit close, don't ya think? I jumped through a lot of hoops to make this happen on air.

WARD
I did the best I could. There were... extenuating circumstances.

JULIE
But his hair... well, we don't have time to get him into makeup. Eh... He's a writer, not an actor. I guess it doesn't matter what he looks like.

PRINTER
That's a bit insulting.

WRITER
Shut your trap.

WARD
(Trying to make him presentable)
Hey! Hey, this lady is just doing her job. The Isaac Asimov award for sci-fi, I mean this is really something.

JULIE
If you wouldn't mind standing over here, Mr. Rinter. I will introduce you in five...

WARD
(to WRITER)
Give me the damn printer.

PRINTER
Where you go, I go.

WRITER
(to WARD)
No!

WARD
Fraternal override.

WARD grabs the PRINTER.

JULIE
Quiet on the set. Camera is rolling and 3, 2, 1... Good evening. Welcome to The New Hottest Thing. I am your host, Julie Marks. Our guest tonight is a man whose first novel is not only a best seller, but a microcosm of the real world. As you know, since "Mechanical Difficulties" hit the shelves, the author has been mysteriously MIA. But he has graciously ended his seclusion tonight, to give his acceptance award. Here. Exclusively for you, loyal fans and readers. It is my great honor and privilege to present the already won but yet unclaimed Isaac Asimov Award for Science Fiction Writing to the spectacular. P. Rinter!
(Applause)
Mr. Rinter, please come on out.

PRINTER
Haha! That's you, dummy!

WARD
Go! That's you!

WRITER enters tenuously to more applause. JULIE hands him the award. WRITER stands there for a moment, fumbling and dumbfounded. He turns to backstage, where both WARD and the PRINTER are urging him to speak.

PRINTER
You forgot our speech, idiot!

WRITER
Um... For a writer, I am suddenly at a loss for words.

PRINTER
Mention me!! Don't forget!

WRITER
I didn't do this alone.

PRINTER
(Sing-songy)
Marshall.... Oh, Marshall...

WRITER
(reacting)
I have many... um... many outside influences.

PRINTER
I am NOT an outside influence.

WRITER
One finds inspiration in the oddest of places and...

PRINTER
Marshall! Tell the truth! You liar! Hypocrite. You disgust me! I'm warning you.

WRITER
I can't do this. You want truth? I'm a fraud!

WRITER runs off stage and grabs the PRINTER from his brother's arms.

WARD
What are you–

WRITER
(returning)
I'll give credit where credit is due. This is the culprit behind my so-called magnificent work! Here she is, world. You can thank P. Rinter!

WRITER holds up the PRINTER for the cameras. JULIE butts in to save the moment, laughing and applauding to cover the awkwardness.

JULIE
Amazing! Simply astonishing how you remain so humble. This is where the magic happens, huh? From your brain to this... What is it, an Epson 6000?

WRITER
No. This. This apparatus here IS the brains behind this operation. She tried to break me. I won't lie. Go on. Tell them. Tell all those beautiful people out there in television land how you spat out this masterpiece entirely on your own!
(NOTHING)
Clamming up, huh?

WRITER opens up a part of the printer and yells into it.

WRITER
I figured as much. Don't tell me you have stage fright, you ball-breaking bitch!

WARD runs on stage, gently trying to escort WRITER off.

WARD
Come on, man, It's all good.
(to the camera and JULIE)
He hasn't slept.

WRITER

I'm a sham! A beard, a front... For a slab of metal. No one wanted me before... Her! Not one of you would have given me the time of day if you were wearing two watches! My lousy agent gave up, and with good reason. I was worse than a washout. I was a never-was. SHE is what you want. Take this award and shove it, you cancerous, malignant monstrosity!

WRITER takes the award and starts beating the PRINTER with it. WARD and JULIE do their best to stop him but WRITER is clearly out of control. WRITER lifts his arm one more time and collapses. JULIE cries to the cameraman.

JULIE

Cut! Cut! Turn off those fucking cameras!

BLACKOUT

SCENE 4

The hospital. WARD is sitting and waiting. The DOCTOR (same actress as JULIE) enters with a lab coat and clipboard. The PRINTER is haphazardly thrown in the corner, with his clothing.

WARD
Have there been any change at all?

DOCTOR
I'm sorry, Mr. Rinter...

WARD
That's not my name! That's not even his name! Didn't they tell you that at triage? What kind of place is this?

DOCTOR
It was very chaotic when they rushed him in. Time is of the essence when there is a catastrophic incident. Especially with a celebrity. Anonymity at this juncture would have been prudent. Now...

WARD
Ward. Just call me Ward. Can I see him?

DOCTOR
Of course, Mr... Ward... But I want you to prepare yourself. He has been like this since his arrival.

The DOCTOR and WARD enter the hospital room. The DOCTOR approaches WRITER who is catatonic in a chair with a blanket over him. He is attached to some apparatus with a cord.

DOCTOR
You have a visitor, Harold.

WARD
His name is Marshall!

WARD (cont.)
(rushing over)
Hey bro, it's me. How are you doing? Mom sends her love. She's home baking a key lime pie. She knows it's your favorite.
(to DOCTOR)
Can he hear me?

WRITER continues to stare blankly ahead.

DOCTOR
Your brother appears to have had a pontine hemorrhage resulting in what we call "locked-in syndrome" He can see and hear, but he is unable to move or respond in any way. Usually, this kind of paralysis happens when there is great trauma to the body, but in this case, we found no medical reason for his condition.

WARD
So, that means he can recover, right?

DOCTOR
At this point, a complete recovery would be highly unusual, but we are hoping he will be able to communicate soon. We have an electronic device that we hope your brother will be able to manipulate with his eyes. Of course, it's too early to try. But do not give up hope, we are making technological advancements every day.

WRITER blinks unseen by anyone.

WARD
You hear that, Marshall? Technology will save you!
(to DOCTOR)
Give it here. I know my brother.

DOCTOR places the machine on WRITER's lap.

WARD
Come on, Marshall. Here's your chance. You can insult me... Tell me

WARD (cont.)
what a jerk I am... I shouldn't have pushed you past your comfort zone. This whole thing is my fault. You are going to be ok. Hey... that hospital johnnie is kinda big on you... Maybe you finally lost that Freshman 15!
(to DOCTOR)
I don't know what I am supposed to say.

DOCTOR
Maybe you could read him the new pages that came in today?

WARD
What?

DOCTOR
The new pages. You are ghost writing his newest book, right? I am riveted. Of course, I loved "Mechanical Difficulties." Read it twice, and I can't wait for the movie. I am such a fan. You really managed to capture his voice in this one.

WARD
What are you talking about?

The DOCTOR grabs some pages from PRINTER, which has been sitting on a side table.

DOCTOR
Chapter 6.

DOCTOR hands WARD the pages. PRINTER reads along with WARD.

WARD
He stared at the vents in the ceiling until they came to life. A parade of cockroaches emerged, covering the walls of the hospital with a single purpose. They scrabbled under the sheet and took residence on Jack's withered body... and waited. Nurse Amy would be in soon to change the bedclothes...

DOCTOR
We have a nurse Amy here. How did you know that?

WARD
Jack could hear the chirping of the roaches, a conspiratorial chorus. But he was powerless to stop the inevitable.

WRITER's eyes begin to flutter wildly.

WARD
Look! Look! He's using the machine.

PRINTER
No... Stop it! Get back in there.

WARD grabs the machine.

WARD
He says, "Unplug me."

PRINTER
No! Don't you dare!

DOCTOR
He has a DNR. You know what this would mean, don't you?

WRITER is blinking. WARD hands back the machine.

WARD
Are you sure?

WRITER blinks wildly.

WARD
He says "Yes." Oh, Marshall. I'll get Mom.

WRITER blinks. WARD reads.

WARD
No. I don't want her here. You do it.

PRINTER
You dirty double-crosser.

WRITER is blinking a lot.

WARD
(Still reading)
My last wish. Break the motherfucking printer.
(to DOCTOR)
He's obviously still delusional.

WRITER begins blinking wildly.

WARD
Ok. Ok. Look, I am taking it to the recycling bin.

DOCTOR
Down the hall to your left. First big door.

PRINTER
Don't think this is the end. Death won't separate us. It will unite us! You good for nothing, dirty thieving swine. You'll melt in hell before I do. I will live again!

WARD exits with the PRINTER. We hear a door close. WRITER begins to blink, then croak out a few words.

WRITER
Th.. Tha.. Thank You.

DOCTOR
Holy Crap! It's a miracle. Don't move. Don't try to speak.

WRITER points to the water and the DOCTOR hands him a cup with a straw.

DOCTOR
Take it easy. Do you know how lucky you are?

WRITER
Lucky...

DOCTOR
If I didn't see this with my own eyes... I am so happy to meet you. I am such a fan of your work.

WRITER
Those days are over.

WARD returns and sees WRITER.

WARD
What?

WARD runs up and hugs WRITER.

WARD
You bastard. You almost had me unplug you.
(to DOCTOR)
He's speaking? Is he going to be ok?

DOCTOR
So hard to know. Can you wiggle your toes?

WRITER
I feel like I could dance the Tarantella.

DOCTOR
I hesitate to say this, but sometimes, these improvements are temporary. We'd like to keep you under observation for a few days, Mr... Marshall. I

DOCTOR (cont.)
need to inform the other doctors. This is quite an astounding phenomenon. I am sure the press would like to interview you...

WRITER
No! No interviews. Never again. Get me out of here. I'll take my chances! Where's the printer?

WARD
You told me to get rid of it. Now you want it back? It's in pieces for recycling.

WRITER
Great. Fantastic.

WRITER unplugs himself from the apparatus. DOCTOR gasps.

WRITER
See, fit as a fiddle. I've seen hell. It's the life I was living. Thanks for everything, Doc, but I am out of here. What do I have to sign?

DOCTOR
You are leaving AMA?

WRITER
Yes! ASAP.

DOCTOR
I'll get the paperwork. In the meantime, would you mind signing my copy of "Mechanical Difficulties?

DOCTOR hands him the book.

WRITER
Fuck no...

WARD
Come on, bro, she probably saved your life. It's the least you can do.

WRITER
FINE. Gimme a pen.

DOCTOR hands him a pen from her clipboard.

WRITER
Hold on to this, because these are the last words I will ever write.

WRITER signs the book as the lights fade.

BLACKOUT

SCENE 5

Sometime later.

NEWSCAST
The world is still buzzing after the very public meltdown, collapse and subsequent disappearance of best-selling author, Marshall Hemmings. After chapters of his unfinished novel, "Transcendental Medications," were found in a garbage can on the Staten Island Ferry, fans speculate Hemmings might have pulled a Spaulding Grey. A makeshift memorial has been established at the site, ironically the opening weekend of the film version of Mechanical Difficulties, which has already brought in $32 million at the box office. The sanitation worker who discovered the chapters will attempt to auction them at Sotheby's next month, if they remain unclaimed by the author, or his estate. Word has it that Hemmings's latest novel paled in comparison to his runaway hit, and the demons that plagued Hemmings from his newfound success proved too much for him to handle. We mourn the loss of another luminous writer, whose light dimmed way too soon.

At rise, WRITER (now MARSHALL) is standing uncomfortably in Copycats Copy Shop in Woonsocket, Rhode Island. The MANAGER is looking over paperwork.

MANAGER
Soooo..... Marshall... You've never worked retail before?

MARSHALL
No.

MANAGER
It appears you have been out of the workforce for a while.

MARSHALL
Yes... I've been... away.

MANAGER
Retired?

MARSHALL
You could say that.

MANAGER
What brings you to Woonsocket, Rhode Island?

MARSHALL
I needed a change of scenery.

MANAGER
Haha. Not much scenery around here. Reservoir is nice, I suppose. The movie theater closed down last month. Mostly the kids hang out in the parking lot of Hal's tire store. Big news is Piggly Wiggly has a special on frozen doughboys this week. Where'd you say you were living?

MARSHALL
Rented a room on Carrington Avenue. It's just a few minutes away.

MANAGER
Not exactly a five-star resort. Mrs. Califano takes in all sorts of riff-raff.

MARSHALL
It's ok. My... um... doctor thought a real change of pace would be good for my head– Er... heart.

MANAGER
Makes no never mind to me. You look clean, and you ain't a felon, right?
(MARSHALL shakes his head "no.")
You ever worked with the Xerox 9000?

MARSHALL
No. But my... (therapist)... I need to expose myself to new technology. Can't be stuck in the past you know...

MANAGER
Well, this here baby is the newest model. Made completely from recycled materials. Energy efficient. Practically runs itself.

MARSHALL nods reluctantly.

MANAGER
We don't get too many customers these days. Most people print their stuff at home. We do high volume jobs. Flyers for lost dogs, garage sales, yoga classes, and the occasional missing person. Stuff like that. It's pretty straightforward. If a customer comes in with an original, it goes in here.

MANAGER demonstrates.

MANAGER
Press the arrow key for the number, green for Go. Luckily, technology still baffles the old folks here. They miss hand-cranked mimeograph machines and carbon paper. Ha-ha!

MARSHALL
Think I can handle it. Green for Go.

MANAGER
And don't forget to smile. Chat them up. If they realize how simple this is, you might be out of a job! Ha-ha. I pay $8.50 an hour, off the books and a 60% discount on office supplies. Comes in handy.

MARSHALL
That's fine.

MANAGER slaps on a name tag or a lanyard.

MANAGER
Well, looks like you are good to go there, Marshall. I'm up to my eyeballs in paperwork. I'll be in my office.

MARSHALL
Thanks. Um...

MANAGER
Call me Sally, honey. And welcome to Copycats.

MANAGER exits. MARSHALL tentatively looks at the machines, taking deep breaths. They can't hurt him, the doctor said. He sits down, perhaps picking up the latest Modern Electronics magazine. After a few beats, CUSTOMER appears. This could be the same actor that plays WARD.

MARSHALL
(forcing a smile)
Welcome to Copycats. How may I help you today?

The CUSTOMER hands him a piece of paper.

MARSHALL (cont.)
Right away, Sir.

MARSHALL (cont.)
Oh... You lost your kitty... Eartha Katt...

CUSTOMER looks annoyed.

MARSHALL (cont.)
Haha! No, sorry. I get it. She's very regal... I hope this helps.

MARSHALL opens the copier.

PRINTER
Why, hello there, Marshall! I've been waiting for you. Where have you been hiding yourself?

MARSHALL slams down the cover. Looks around. CUSTOMER is still standing there, has heard nothing. MARSHALL lifts the cover again.

PRINTER
Still here, baby. Ask him how many copies he needs, handsome.

MARSHALL
(on automatic pilot)
How many copies do you need, handsome?

CUSTOMER
What??

MARSHALL
(snapping out)
I mean...

CUSTOMER
(slightly offended)
35 should do.

MARSHALL
So sorry, I...

PRINTER
Don't worry. I got this.

PRINTER begins churning out papers. They start flying everywhere.

MARSHALL
(defeated)
Yeah. I got this.

MARSHALL starts collecting the papers that are flying around him as the lights fade.

END OF PLAY

More plays by Bambi Everson

Visit BambiEverson.com

Also available in paperback

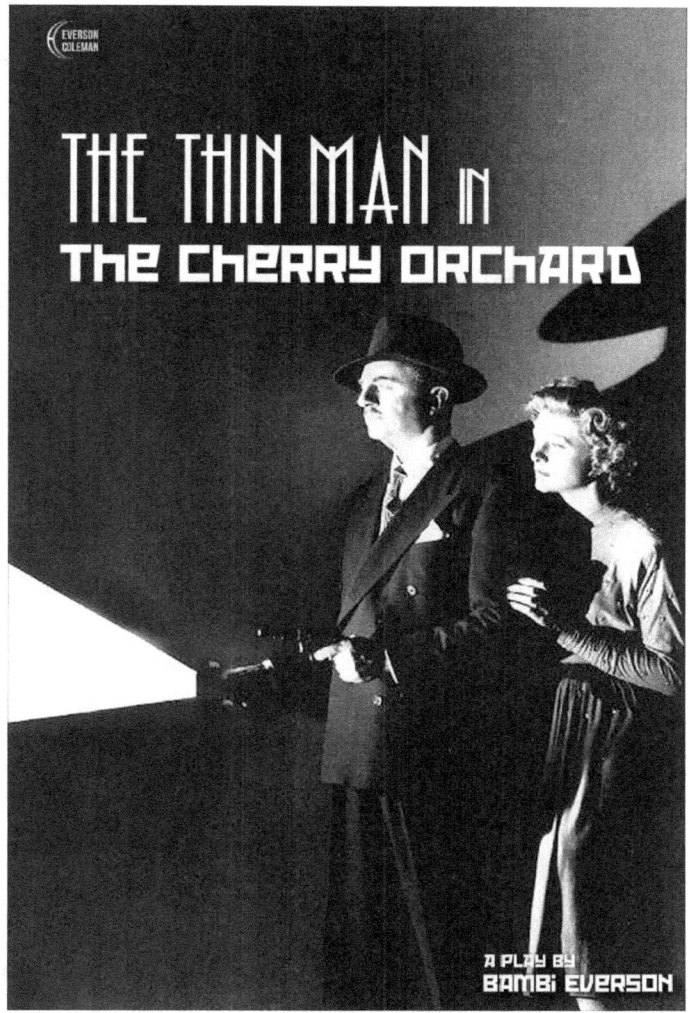

THE THIN MAN IN THE CHERRY ORCHARD

In this sardonic mashup, Dashiell Hammett's hard-boiled, glamorously pickled American sleuths, Nick and Nora Charles, meet their cousins, the stoic inhabitants of Chekhov's bleak Russian tundra. Naturally, a murder, and hilarity, ensues. Can Nick solve the crime before they run out of vodka? Full length, approximately 100 minutes, one optional intermission. Comedy-Mystery. 4M, 4F.

Also available in paperback

NICK AND NORA GO OFF-BROADWAY

In this standalone sequel to The Thin Man in the Cherry Orchard, Anya convinces Nora to take part in an amateur theater production. As is par for the course, a murder takes place and Nick must solve the crime before opening night. Full length, approx. 100m, one intermission. Comedy-Mystery, 5M, 3F.

Also available in paperback

FINDING ANDREW
Twelve-year-old Virginia's peculiar connection to Andrew is met with uncertainty and doubt by her best friend, Max. One act, approx. 22 minutes. Drama. 1F, 2 teens (M/F)

DAD'S HOME
Paul is home from the office. Something is terribly wrong, and everybody knows but him. One act, approx. 50 minutes. Drama. 2M, 1F, 1M teen.

Also available in paperback

SINCERELY HELD BELIEFS

Mandy is caught between her two friends. One a grieving mother, and the other a zealous clairvoyant who is convinced she is receiving messages from the other side. Mandy must try to mediate these two relationships, while staying true to her own beliefs. Full length, approx. 80 minutes. Psychological Drama. 3F, 20s-40s. Trigger warning: child death.

Also available in paperback

MURDER IS SERVED
A murderous love triangle amongst octogenarians in an assisted living facility. Married for 40 years, Steve Lowenthal's life has been made intolerable by his henpecking wife, Rita. Finding new love in the rehabilitation center leads to deceit, treachery, revenge and cheating at Scrabble. One act, approx. 45 minutes. Dark Comedy. 2F, 2M.

DECEPTION
A brief encounter in a bar leads to a complicated entanglement. Dishonesty and lying are rampant, but who is doing what? One act, approx. 55 minutes. Drama/Mystery. 2F, 2M.

Bambi Everson

ABOUT THE AUTHOR

Bambi Everson is a playwright, actor, and teaching artist. Her full-length, THE THIN MAN IN THE CHERRY ORCHARD had a sold out run at the 2019 New York Fringe Festival, and is among a growing series of her plays available in paperback from The Drama Book Shop and Amazon. Her work has also been produced at Manhattan Repertory Theatre, Hudson Guild, Emerging Artists Theatre, The Little Theatre of Alexandria, VA, and college productions in North Carolina and Arkansas.

She studied with Geraldine Page and Michael Schulman, and appeared in many Off-Off Broadway productions in her youth. She wrote her first play in 2015, and has since completed over 30 more, including six full lengths.

Her work tends to incorporate oddball characters and situations. Subject matter has ranged from screwball comedy to dark melodrama, from cannibals in suburban Long Island, to blind dates with bearded ladies. She's been influenced as much by cinema as she has by theater, an inescapable accident of birth, as she's the daughter of noted film historian, William K. Everson.

She was the recipient of the 2015 Yip Harburg Foundation award. She teaches playwriting in Manhattan, and is a member of Actors' Equity Association and The Dramatist's Guild.

Follow her adventures at her website, bambieverson.com

www.ingramcontent.com/pod-product-compliance
Lightning Source LLC
LaVergne TN
LVHW051844080426
835512LV00018B/3060